I would like to give a big thankyou to my dearest son Arthur Matthews, daughter Diana Matthews and best friend Chris Farrugia for their continued support and encouragement to produce this book

Photography the nuts and bolts!

By Simon James Matthews LBIPP

Me with super model Caprice Bourret

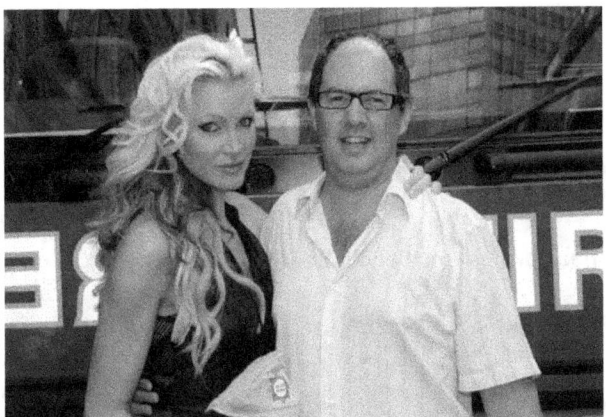

I would like to dedicate this book to my grandad
James Ball. (Pop) I Love you and will always miss you

Contents

Introduction:

Do you love photography? Wish you could make money from it? Want to turn your hobby into a passive income.

You can do all the above, and with this guide I will show you how.

Why me? I have over 40 years of photography experience. From, shooting over 2000 weddings, to working for world-class media agencies, I have a stock library with more than 100000 images So, with me, you will be learning from a true self-made expert.

This guide is therefore produced to equip you with all the knowledge to get straight into the action! You will be led through how to build an image library, expand your photography skills with great tips and short cuts that will save you years in the industry. My straight-to-the-point method skips all the technical jargon that you do not need but talks you through all the essentials; from the basics of getting the exposure right, to the art of catch-flash, top tips on what to shoot, where to shoot and maximise the output from any form of photography.

So, what are you waiting for?
The sooner you start reading the better!

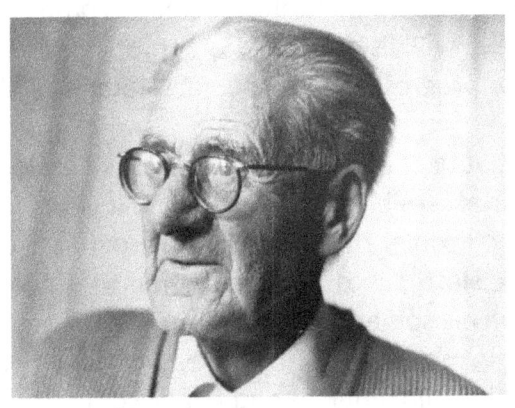

My Grandad James Ball (Pop);
who this book is dedicated to, and who
resides forever in my memory

1 Who should read this Book?

So, the big question in hand is who should buy and read this book? Well, this book is made to be accessible to anyone with the slightest interest in photography. Photography is accessible to everyone. Everyone can try their hand at stock photography and videography. Even those with only a reasonable mobile phone. Honestly, you do not need fancy equipment, but I will elaborate on this later. In terms of knowledge, you only really need basic computer skills, and we will discuss the photography basics, and how to progress in these subjects later as well.

The real beauty of photography is that, like I said before, it is accessible to everyone, and it is completely flexible. This means it is a great passion that can be slotted into your spare time. Photography is something that you can do at any opportunity, meaning it can work easily around your work, relationship, hobbies and family commitments. For example, days out and special events with family and friends tend to be the perfect moments for pictures, and a good portion of those pictures could be stock suitable, helping you to increase the size of your image library.

Personally, it has taken me over ten years to fine-tune my stock photography. Which is why I am here to help you. With this book and my method, you can save that dead-space time and find yourself earning that extra income from photography much sooner than you thought. Wouldn't it be nice to start creating an image library that continues to expand and can provide extra income for the coming years? The insane thing about these image libraries is that they can provide income for limitless years the images never expire! Therefore, it is completely in your hands as to how far you want to go with your photography. There are no limitations, and this book can be used to work through at your own pace and to fit in with your own lifestyle. But believe me when I say, I wish I had started doing this 30 years ago.

Therefore, my advice to you? Start reading this book and start taking those photographs. The sooner you start the better. I will outline my main methodology for stock photography and the shortcuts that I have learnt through decades of hard graft. These will help you fine tune your photography skills and start making money from your hobby.

What will we cover?

This book will cover everything you need to know to make money from photography. We will go through the basics, like how to take a perfect photograph and the technical aspects of using a camera (shutter speed anyone?). Then, I will recommend the best micro stock images sale sites to get you started with your stock library. Finally, there is an overview and breakdown of how the image companies work, so you can fully understand the structure of the company, the keywords to use on your images, how the payment system works and, most importantly, what the earning potential from this is.

I will show you amazing shortcuts to help you optimise the outcomes from your images and video clips. Tricks that I have learned over the years, designed to save you time and enlarge your image collection, and therefore your earning potential, faster. We will discuss what is a desirable photo from a stock point of view. Therefore, you will know what to take pictures of and what to avoid. You will then know what is meant by a commercial image.

We will look at basic camera functions. Explaining things like how does depth of field work, how to shoot on manual, what is ISO? And how it affects quality, file sizes explained, benefits of shooting Raw or Jpeg. We will also look at shooting video clips and I will give you some basic tips. I will teach you in a practical and methodical way step by step.
But do not worry as this book is not about filling your head full of technical jargon. This is a practical book, and I will explain things in a simple, informative and practical way, making it very easy and fun to learn and understand.

Now there will also be sections on Wedding Photography, Commercial and Press work.

These will be relatively short but will contain some particularly good tips hopefully with time, you will be able to expand your abilities and your portfolio. Or maybe you are already an experienced or a keen amateur, in which case these sections will be useful with straight forward tips, hopefully you will follow my methodical way of working.

What is Stock photography?

There are many forms of photography, Weddings, Portraiture, Commercial, Press and Stock. So, what is "Stock Photography" and how does it work? There are many online companies now that specialize in supplying stock images and video clips.
The basic format is straightforward enough, these companies have huge data bases containing millions of stock images, of different varieties and cover just about everything in life you could think off. These images are supplied and uploaded by people like me, possibly you, the images are then held in your portfolio and on their image library. Companies, people and picture buyers from all around the world will search this library, find the image they require, purchase it in the format and with the license they require. (I will go into detail about licenses later) You are then paid a royalty based on the format for that company. Every time one of your images is purchased you get a royalty, and you will receive a royalty every single time your image is purchased

forever! Now a simple principle, the more images you have in your portfolio the more you will make. I will show you through this book how to build a huge library of images in a short time. Using the skills and tricks that I have fine-tuned over the last ten years or so.

2 Do I need professional equipment?

I get asked this question time and time again. Often, people say things like "Oh, I can't be a photographer or make money from my photography, as I don't have the correct equipment to shoot decent enough images". Well, that is where you are wrong.

You absolutely do not need to have expensive, "professional" equipment. Now, I am not saying that obtaining high-quality, and therefore most likely expensive, equipment may not help you to obtain better images. The higher end equipment may, in fact, give you more options and flexibility for the scope and type of images you can take. Which can, in turn, help increase your range of photos and improve your income. However, believe it or not, it is not imperative to have this equipment. Especially not at the initial stage. With the advances in technology, it is now much easier to obtain good images with a compact camera, or even a mobile phone.
There are huge limitations to using smart phones do not get me wrong, but I will outline these later. I have uploaded and sold images, directly taken from my smartphone and it is a good way to start out if you do not have anything else available. Later, hopefully you will be able to buy something more useful like a good compact camera, nowadays for a couple of hundred dollars you can buy some genuinely nice and extremely capable photographic equipment. I will go into more detail about the

equipment, the pros, and the con's and give a few examples later. You may of course already have reasonable photographic equipment, in that case all well and good read my book and crack on!

Does it matter where I live?

This is another one of those questions! "I can't do stock photography there is nothing to take pictures of where I live" NO! NO! NO! It makes absolutely no difference where you live!
I can tell you now that huge amounts of stock images are sold every hour around the world, of everyday life and objects! You can live anywhere on this planet, and I can tell you without a shadow of doubt there are literally millions of things you could take pictures of hundreds in fact in your own home. Just look around you right now. What do you see? maybe a laptop, coffee cup with a plate and a sandwich on it, notebook and pen, and a mobile phone next to it that is just in front of you while you are reading this book.

This is stock. These are pictures that will sell and sell again and again. And this is just at your table! It is what is in front of me right now as I type, look around while you are reading this book, I bet if you think and look carefully you could probably see loads of possible pictures right in front of your nose?

Here is another example of an easy picture that you could take, I was simply walking along a stony beach with my daughter, and I asked her to lay down with her eyes closed like she was listening to her iPod. Bingo another stock image, why is this a good stock image? Because it involves leisure and relaxing, plus she is using an iPod, that's technology. Was it hard to take this picture? No, it was not, I was out for the day anyway with my family and there you go a nice stock image produced, that will sit in my library for ever. Who knows how much it will earn over years, £25, £50 maybe hundreds! In the end of the day if I did not take this picture and it was not added to my library, I would not earn anything so there is nothing to lose. You can do the same.

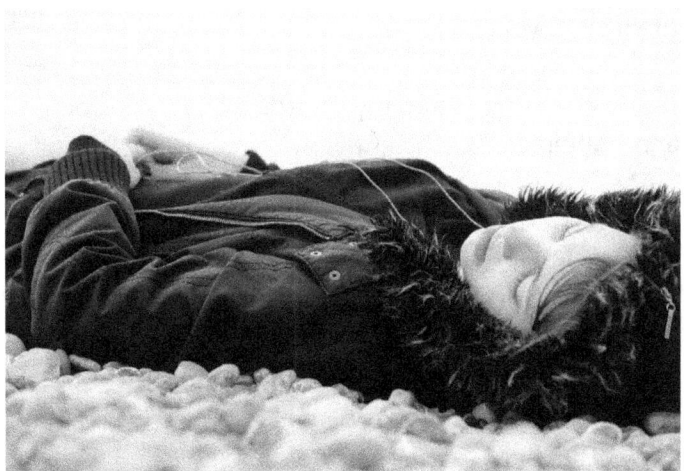

I get so annoyed when people say there is nothing around me to take lovely pictures of, there is you just need to think, look and follow the tips in this book, and it will become second nature to you. Eventually you will see good stock pictures everywhere, wherever you are whatever you are doing in fact, and that is just doing everyday life things, what about what is around the corner from you? Maybe a nice church? A park, fields, buildings, seaside resorts, cafe's the list is endless, and the possibilities are endless believe me, and I show you how to get 100's of images from even one subject in one hour!

Once you start planning what and how to shoot the possibilities are endless and this is what I am going to show you how to do. I will show you how to get the most from what you shoot, with my knowledge that I have built up being a professional photographer over the last 10 years.

Now I have fine-tuned my photography to perfection and unbelievably efficiently. When you go to shoot a scene for instance of a church let us just say, I will show you how to turn what you would probably think is 20 images at the most into 200! And with these skills you will build your image library in no time at all, and it will just grow and grow and give you an income for years and years! And the more you put into it the more you will get out. But take my advice start now as soon as possible I wished I started properly with it 30 years ago! And I wished I had thought about it more carefully all those years ago because the last five years have really made a massive difference on how I shoot and work today. I probably would have 10 million images out there now if I had thought about it more carefully.

But do not give up your day job just yet, it takes time this is not a get rich quick idea, certainly not, but if done the right way you can certainly get to where you want to be and like a said before, the great thing is it will fit in perfectly with what you are already doing.

Equipment and basic technics

This section covers equipment and basic technicalities, what things are and what they do, like Shutter Speed, Aperture, Focus, Auto and Manual shooting, ISO and so on. I will talk about some certain models and manufactures as examples and give some basic instructions and a quick tutorial on using them, getting the best out of them and what is achievable and what could be their limitations. But these tips will apply to remarkably similar types and models of equipment so if you have something similar, it should help you.

So, what are some basic features that you will find on most compact and medium spec cameras? What do they do? And how to use them.

First some basics on how we get a reasonable picture on any camera or mobile phone in fully auto mode, or basically when you just click the button or shutter release on a camera, and you end up with a reasonable looking image on the screen.

What are the factor's that produced that nice looking bright image? Once you understand what is required to get a usable image it will help you later how to change things manually and experiment. Then you will be able take pictures in manual mode to get a desired effect for the picture depending on the subject you are shooting. We are not talking about composition here that will come later.

So the three main factor is that produce that image, are called the "Golden Triangle". They are ISO, aperture and shutter speed settings. When you click the shutter button three things need to work together to produce a correctly exposed image. So, what do I mean by "exposed" when we take a picture, we need the camera to adjust certain things to get the correct exposure, exposure is the amount of light that enters the lens and is then exposed to the censer on the camera, (in the old days that would be the negative film) which is then saved in a file format to the memory card.

If the exposure is wrong for any reason, the image taken can be very dark or very bright, in effect unusable depending on how wrong the exposure is. Some minor exposure errors can be adjusted in software post taking the picture but for me I try to get the exposure as perfect as possible straight away in the camera, this makes for good practice. I will go into this later. When the camera operates in fully auto mode it will adjust these three things to try to obtain the best exposure. Also, the camera will auto focus, which will in theory give you a sharp image as it will automatically focus the lens correctly on the subject. But I will go onto the focus later, for now we are concentrating on getting the correct exposure.

Now if this combination of shutter speed, aperture and ISO are set correctly by the automation of the equipment for light that is available, you should pretty much get a nicely exposed usable image. In most cases the camera will do a good job and get a good image, but not always, although camera equipment is very advanced and sophisticated now, it can be fooled very easily. I will explain later how this happens.

(See three example images)

First image is over exposed, too much light, washed out looking image.

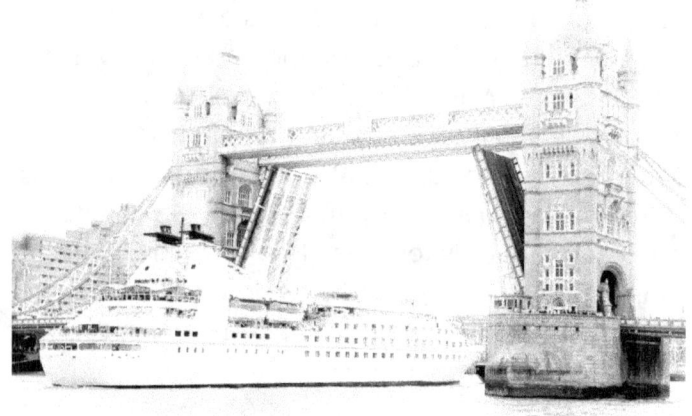

Next image is under exposed. Not enough light, dark.

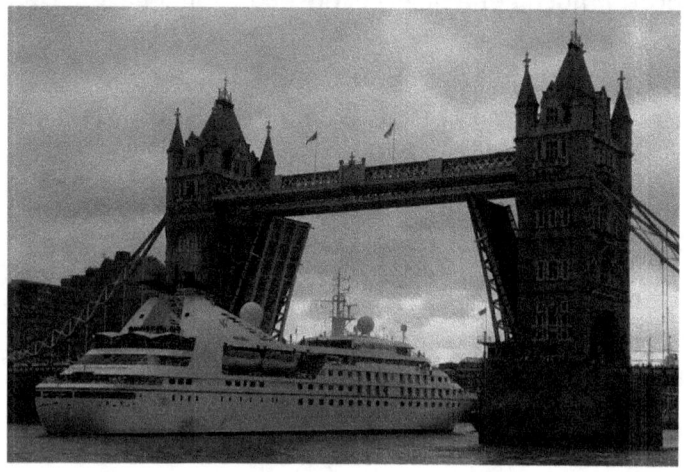

Last, correctly exposed image.

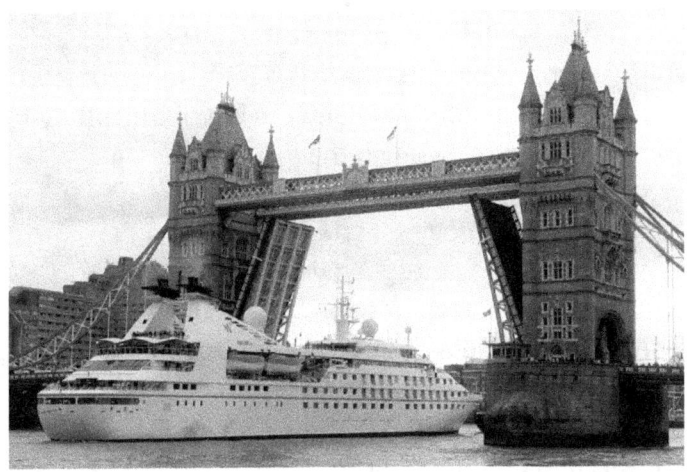

Now I will explain the details of these three primary functions. Once you learn about these functions and what they do you will be able to shoot in semi - automatic mode or fully manual instead of just fully automatic.

Shutter speed control

Shutter and speed control are often a topic that confuses many people. There is a large range of shutter types in different cameras but, luckily, they all operate in pretty much the same way.

The shutter is a moving part of the camera that opens and closes at a speed you or, if you are in auto-mode, the camera sets. Speeds used range from as slow as less than $1/20^{th}$ of a second, to as fast as $1/8000^{th}$ of a second (which is extremely fast).

For this book I will try and keep things as easy as possible. To use shutter speed correctly, you must first consider the purpose of the photograph. And then the use.

Let us take a simple example:
If you wanted to take a picture of fast-moving objects such as birds flying, or even people playing sport, you would need to use a fast shutter speed. An example of this would be using $1/1000^{th}$ for a moving car.

A fast shutter speed allows the image to be frozen, simply put, the faster the shutter speed, the higher the camera's capability of freezing a moving subject object in your photograph.

There may be occasions when a slower shutter speed is more desirable when photographing fast moving objects. This is known as a "panning" with the subject. If performed correctly, you can obtain a clear image of the main subject (i.e., the car), with a nice blurry focus in the background. This is often used to give a desired effect of speed.

Here I have panned the camera with a shutter speed of 125th of a sec, as you can see the subject the man riding the bicycle is nice and sharp, but the background is blurry which gives you the impression of speed

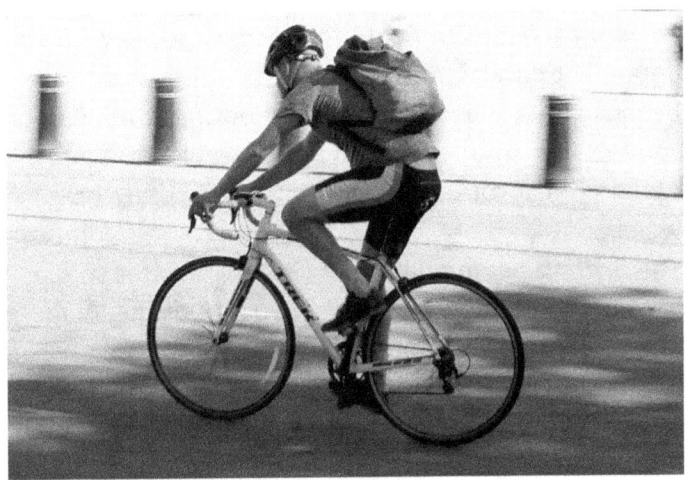

"Panning" does take practice. And a lot of it. However, when done correctly, it can result in a stunning effect which gives one the fantastic sense of speed in a 2D photograph.

Aperture control:

Now we move on to Aperture control, the lens on your camera and mobile phone controls the light entering the lens by what is called the aperture, these are blades near the front of the lens that close and open depending on the settings of the camera. They will range from something like f1.2 to f22; other than controlling the amount of light entering the lens the aperture also controls the depth of field of the image you are capturing.

So, what is depth of field? This is an especially important part of photography to understand, because later when you will be shooting in manual or semi-manual mode you will be controlling the depth of field to capture the image in the way that you want.
This with the combination of ISO and shutter speed, is what gives you the correct exposure of the image and give you the effect you want to have.

This is the difference between shooting in auto-mode where the camera makes the decisions. Once you have an understanding on how these factors work and work together, you will become a much better photographer and you will not be just pointing and shooting.

These two things Shutter speed and aperture control are only a small part of the factors in taking better pictures, but they are pretty much the most important by far. Once you master the use of them correctly your photography will improve dramatically.

So, some detail on how depth of field works: I will try to explain this in the easiest way as possible, with some examples for you to look at, it is very straight forward to grasp.

First the simple principle is that when you select a low f-stop say f1.8 or f2.8 the aperture on the lens opens very wide you are letting a lot of light through the lens at near its widest part. This will give what we call a shallow depth of field. Where the main subject will be clear, in focus and the background will be much less. Now, depending on the lens type this effect can be more dramatic. Telephoto lenses like 300mm or higher have a very extreme depth of field, so shooting at f1.8 for instance blurs the background more than a standard 50mm.

Now the other end of the spectrum, changing the f-stop aperture setting on the lens, to say f16 or f22 this will have the reverse effect. When the picture is taken the lens aperture will close exceedingly small, like a tiny pin whole. In an image this will give the effect that the depth of focus will be much further in front and behind the focus point of the image. These

elements of aperture control will have an instant effect on your picture capabilities. For instance, let us say you were doing a portrait session for someone, and they just wanted a head and shoulders type image. The background is not that relevant to the image, so you could use a small aperture like f1.8 to keep the background out of focus to a certain degree as much as possible.
On the other extreme, if you were taking a portrait of someone standing with a lovely mountain range in the background, you would use as high f-stop as possible like f16 so that all that beauty will be sharp. Please see the examples to show you how depth of field and aperture work:

Examples of depth of field:

First image, shallow depth of field, very open aperture, f1.8

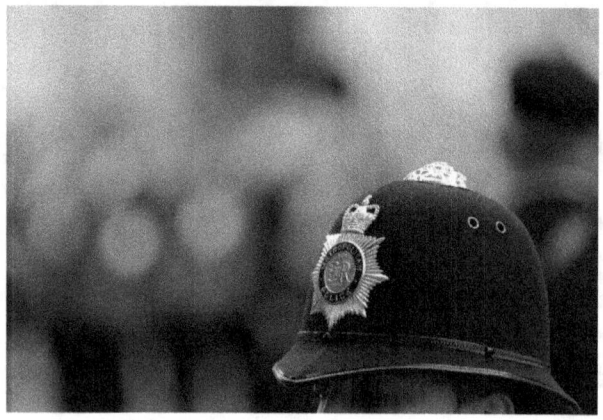

Next, high depth of field. f22

Notice how everything in the image is very sharp from the close part, the actual sign to the very top of the building.

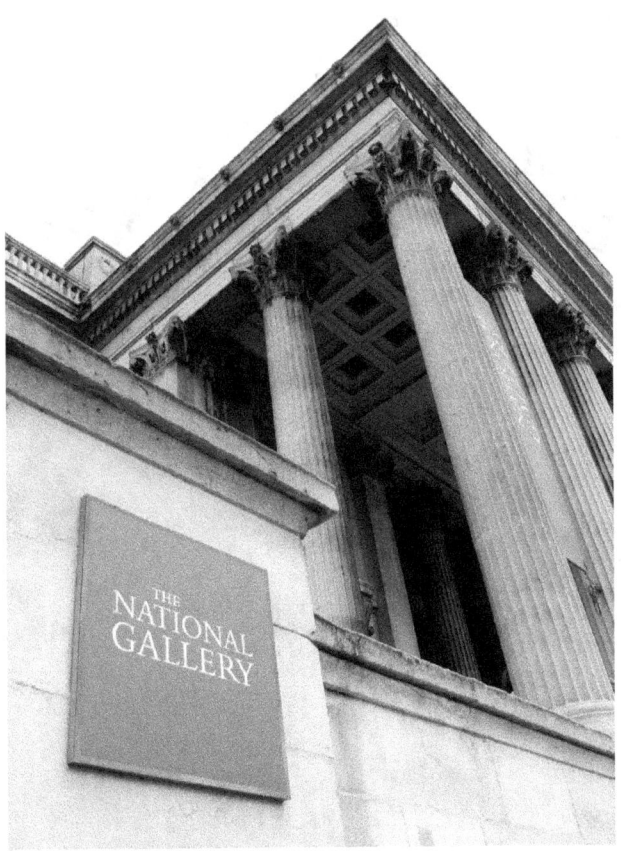

Another good example, f22 amazing depth in this image

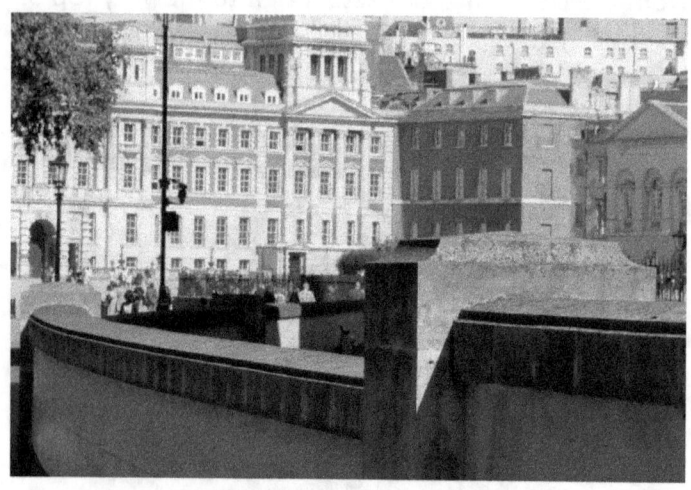

ISO explained

I am going to talk about the other setting from the golden triangle the ISO, what does it do? And how will it affect your images and other factors.
First what does ISO stand for? The initials stand for "International Organization of Standardization", which is the main governing body that standardizes sensitivity ratings for camera sensors. This term was carried over from using film in cameras when the ISO rating was known as the "film speed" and ASA. (ASA stands for American Standards Association)

So, what does ISO do? ISO effects the sensitivity of the camera's sensor, in plain and simple terms a higher ISO setting will make the sensor more sensitive to light. Thereby when you set the ISO on higher numbers the sensors need less light to capture the image. So, in darker conditions like sunrise or night-time you in theory can use a remarkably high ISO so that you can take an image without the need of a tripod for instance. Now then the ISO setting will directly affect what settings you will need to get the correct exposure, i.e., shutter speed and aperture. When the camera is set in fully automatic mode, normally it will use a high ISO number, so that in turn the camera can select faster shutters speeds and higher aperture numbers. This way it will help to eliminate camera shack for one thing and create a sharp image. That is what the manufactures want the equipment to do straight out of the box and in auto mode. In turn using exceptionally low ISO settings like 100 which is normally the lowest, the cameras sensor will require lots of light to capture the image, therefore you will have less flexibility when selecting shutter speed and aperture as these directly affect the light which reaches the sensor. Now you could conclude, well fine I will just use an extremely high ISO setting or leave my camera to select the best ISO in auto mode. But you should be aware that high ISO settings effect the quality of the image. On some equipment on extremely high ISO settings the image produced can be granny and noisy. With lower priced equipment this is more prominent, as you go higher up the price range it becomes less of a problem, some professional models are capable of shooting on extremely high ISO settings and still giving excellent quality images. In general, I will always try to shoot with the lowest ISO setting I can, this way you can be assured of the best quality image being produced.

Here is a good **Top Tip** that is missed a lot by would be photographers, look through your camera settings you should find a section on "**Image noise reduction**". By default, most cameras will have this set on normal, but it should have choices like low, high or medium. I always change this to the highest setting so it would be set to high. This can slow the processing speed of the camera down, because as soon as you take a picture the camera will process the image on the highest noise reduction setting, trying to eliminate as much noise or grain in the processes system as possible. When doing stock photography this is not an issue as you are not interested in shooting 10 frames in a second like a sports photographer would be. So always set it to highest level possible and it will help a tremendous amount with the quality of the images especially when using higher ISO settings.

But remember if you want to shoot lots of frames at an extremely fast rate then turn the Image noise reduction back down to low or medium, so that your camera image processing can keep up with the number of frames you are taking. On more expensive equipment this tends not to be so much of an issue as they can process large amounts of images. So, you can keep the image noise reduction on high all the time. But for medium and low-end equipment adjusting this setting can really help with image quality when shooting on high ISO settings. It is often overlooked by a lot of photographers.

White Balance:

Now this subject can cause a lot of problems for keen amateurs. The white balance (WB) correction on most digital cameras will work well just left on the auto setting. It is a system designed to correct unrealistic colour cast, so that objects that are meant to be white in your images will appear white, colour cast effect can come from many sources and can affect the whole image. So, for instance if you were shooting a portrait session in a room that had predominately red coloured walls the chances are your pictures would come out with a strong tint of red all over.

The WB systems considers the warmth or coolness of the white light that is available. You can correct WB errors by adjusting the settings manually. WB is measured in something called Kelvin. And ranges from 1000 -1000K.
As a rough guide for instance when using a flashgun your camera will automatically set the K (WB) between 5000-5500K. Daylight with a clear sky and sunlight overhead will be anything from 5000K to 6500K. You will find settings on your camera to represent certain conditions where you can set the WB to stay on that setting, for instance using flash. It is very handy to experiment with this adjustment as there can be times when you want to override the auto setting and make slight adjustments depending on the lighting conditions present. For most of the

time though the cameras auto setting will do a surprisingly good job. Just keep an eye out for whites looking white in the image. If they are tinted in anyway this will be an instant indication that the auto setting is not correct, and you can adjust as required. I normally look at what the camera tells me it thinks the WB should be, then if the images look wrong adjust it up or down depending on whether the images look to warm or to cool.

You can purchase WB metres that work well, but you only require one if you are shooting a lot in studios or with very mixed lightening.

Recap:

Now we have a basic understanding of the three factors or "Golden Triangle" that control image exposure that is getting the image exposed correctly for a nice picture.

You should understand how the three factors, shutter speed, aperture and ISO work together to obtain the correct exposure. As now you understand how these three factors can affect the image you will be able to practice the different combinations to see the effects, they have on the image captured.

But if you want to start shooting in manual mode rather than automatic you must get the right combination of shutter speed, aperture and ISO to get the correct exposure. We will now move onto the exciting world of shooting in manual or semi manual mode, which will open a whole new world of photographic possibilities for you, so your artist talents can shine through.

But before I do the other thing that I mentioned earlier in this section was focus. This is controlled by the camera in auto mode, or you can set it to manual.

Now nearly all modern cameras have very sophisticated auto focus systems, with multi point focus selection, face recognition, focus taking sometimes with up to 50 selectable focus points. I personally rarely shoot in manual focus mode, it is never really required, the only time I use manual focus is maybe doing long exposure night-time photography. The camera you are using will without a doubt have an extremely efficient focus systems. Most cameras use similar systems, and you will have to experiment with you own equipment to get the best out of it. In general, most will have several focusing points that the camera will use to focus on the subject. Now you can normally move the focus point to the area that you want to focus on, and the camera will lock onto this object. Then the camera will let you take the picture once it is locked into focus. I am not going to go into too much depth in this book about focus control as just experimenting with your own camera settings will be the best way forward.

One thing I will mention though, is look through your camera settings and look for one shot focusing or tracked focusing. The two choices should be called something like that. This choice is relevant as it will affect your pictures dramatically, as you do not want out of focus images! So, the basic system is this, one shot focusing is for a static subject, like for instance a person standing in front of a beautiful scene like mountains. When you are taking pictures of static scenes you want the focus point set on one shot, so that the camera focuses on the subject and stays focused on it to take the photograph. This you will be doing continuously stop in stock photography. The other choice is tracked focus, or focus tracking, here the camera will focus on a moving subject for instance like a car and then it will track that object to stay in focus. In this case that is exactly what you want. Like photographing a racing car around a racetrack. Play around with your camera focus settings to get the best out of it. Another common and useful feature on your camera will be "focus lock" here you will point the camera at the subject that you want in focus push the button slightly but do not take the picture, let the camera focus, then push and hold the focus lock button, then re-frame your picture and take the shot. Here the camera will stay focused on the initial focus point and stay focused on that, even though you have re-framed the shot. Therefore, you are directly controlling the focus point and telling the camera to stay on that point, very handy if you want to take a scene for instance of something awfully close to you but slightly out of the main focusing point and you want this to be sharp. Not all compact cameras have this feature, but a lot will have.

3 Getting the right exposure:

Shooting in manual mode:

We have now looked at the three main factors that are shutter speed, aperture and ISO which will determine the correct exposure for the image. Now I will teach you an easy way to use your camera in manual mode and get the exposure for the image correct. This is a learning process that over time will become easier.

The best way to start is to take a picture of anything, when you look through the view finder and slightly press the shutter release button, with the camera in auto mode the camera should display in the view finder the settings for the light conditions that are available. Therefore, if you look at these settings in the view finder you should see what the camera believes will be the correct shutter speed and aperture for this photograph. Now all you must do is remember these two settings, switch your camera to manual, set the shutter speed and aperture by using the menus on the camera to what you saw in the view finder. Then take the picture, so what you have done now you have used a cameras automated system to give you what it believes are the correct settings to expose the image correctly. But you have set the camera on manual and taken the image with those settings. Furthermore, you can now look at the image you have just taken, decided whether it looks correctly exposed, if it does not you can adjust manually to correct it.

This way you will learn how to correct under and over exposed images. So, what is meant by over or under exposed? This is the easy part, a picture that is over exposed will be too bright, it will look washed out with very bright areas, some cameras will have a setting called highlights which will be displayed on the back when viewing the image. You may have to look at your camera menus to switch this feature on. When on the displayed image will flash area's that are too bright, they will normally flash or pulse. If an image is under exposed, it will appear to dark. Now once you are aware that the exposure is wrong by either being too bright or to dark you can manually adjust your settings for either shutter speed, by reducing the shutter speed to a slower setting therefore letting more light in, which will brighten the image, or set it faster to reduce the amount of light entering therefore making the image darker. The same process is used for the aperture settings, lager aperture numbers will make the image darker or lower numbers will let more light in making the image brighter. Now you can see that by adjusting either of these two settings you can get the correct exposure. Also, as you become more experienced you will be able to adjust your camera settings to get the affects you require, like depth of field or freezing moving subjects. By experimenting you will soon be able to shoot in manual mode fully and get the best image you can under the light conditions and the subject you are shooting.

There are other in camera aides to help get the correct exposure depending on your camera, most have a display called a " Histogram " this is a display like a bare graph that you can look at which will tell you how much light has been exposed and by looking at the graph you can access if an equal or evenly spread histogram is shown, Which will indicate that the image is exposed correctly. I will not go into too much detail about this in this book, but I do cover it detail in my further books. Now as we have talked about ISO and how it effects how much light is needed for the censor to record the image, you can start to set your ISO on manual and adjust it according to the lightning condition that you are shooting in and the shutter speed or aperture you require to obtain the effect or type of picture you want. You will see by raising the ISO it will give you more flexibility in choosing the other two factures, Shutter speed and aperture. I normally set my ISO at 400 and work from there going down or up as required. But I rarely go above 1000 even with my most expensive camera. Because no matter how good it is, I still feel that keeping my ISO lower will always give me the best quality. Now of course it does depend on what you are shooting and for what purpose, when I am shooting Press stuff like politicians or a news story, I am happy to go as high as necessary in order to keep my shutter speed as high as possible, one thing I do not want is blurry images. Better to have a loss of quality and have a bit of grain then an unusable picture because it is blurry. But for stock purposes using ISO at around 400 will give you plenty of flexibly with your combination of shutter speed and aperture.

Conclusion:

Now armed with these fundamentals of getting the correct exposure, using shutter and aperture control you can spend time practicing and experimenting. Have fun with it and see the different effects these controls have over the images you take.
For a complete guide on camera settings in detail please refer to my other publications.

What should I shoot?

What should you be shooting? What are commercial images? What types of images sell well? What not to shoot? These are the questions that everybody getting into stock photography will ask. It is a big subject, and I am going to try to help you as much as possible. Of course, depending on where you live could be a big factor in determining what you can shoot? However, believe me you will be able to find great stock images for your library wherever you live, they are in fact all around you! look in front of you right now? What do you see? A coffee table with a coffee cup on and some papers? A plant and my book. This is a viable commercial image that can sell. People buy images like this all the time, again and again, because the digital market for stock images is so vast it is hard to believe. You see someone maybe making a website about studying for instance and they need a stock picture showing a laptop, keyboard with some notes in front on a coffee table. That is your image right there! Take a picture right now of what is in front of you! Take a few at different angles, before you know it you will have a collection of 10 images from just in front of you!

Now with your knowledge of ISO, shutter and aperture control you can get the best of any scene. Try to improve the light in room.

One thing that is important for most stock images is getting the light constant and spread evenly.
There are occasions when harsh light does look good. But these are more artistic looking images. For basic stock pictures of pretty much anything. Good bright, evenly lit is best and will sell more regular.
Commercial images are images that people, bloggers, companies, schools and colleges will use again and again when creating something online or in print. Start with anything on your doorstep. Look around the house? What is outside? Around the corner? Maybe you have a busy market near where you live? Pictures of people walking around markets, trading or buying, looking at clothes and food on stalls are always popular. These types of images should be wide giving a general view rather than specific person buying something.

Now as I am mentioning people and places let us take this opportunity to briefly talk about license types and classifications of images type. Licences are what the company holding your images on will issue to someone buying your image, the licence will determine the price for the image and use for that image.

There are two main classifications for images, none-editorial and editorial. What are the differences and how do I use them in my stock photography?

Keeping it simple a none-editorial image will have no visible trademarks, like an Apple Logo, if it has recognizable people in it, you will need a model release forms for each one giving permission to use their image.

An editorial image on the other had can have virtually anything in it, brand names, people face, shop brands and clothing brands. There are a few buildings and landmarks around the world where you really cannot even use the building or area for editorial images.

Some large national parks for instance you may need permission to take pictures, always check if you are unsure.

Editorial images can have pretty much any branding in them or people as they are only meant to be used for editorial purposes, i.e., someone writing an article on markets for example, they can use an image with people in, shops stalls, branding logos because the image is only being used for a one-off article about that subject. So editorial classifications give you a huge scope for images of everyday life, which is good for stock purposes.

Non-editorial images on the other hand can be used for advertising, that is why they would need a model release form from anyone in the picture or permissions from any branded company visible in the image.

Getting the most from what is around you

When you are out and about, around interesting locations you need to get the best out of what is available. Here I will discuss how to make the most from a location and turn what you would think is just 10 pictures into a 100!

Let us just say you have a local centre point of interest in your town, with maybe a fountain, a couple of statues and a market.
To start with you would probably take quite a few what would be called general views, wide shots of cafés, people milling around, shopping maybe a few statues something like that. This is all fine. But you need to look further and think about what else you get out of this location. For instance, when I take a photograph of a statue, yes you can take a full-length picture showing the statues, maybe a wide shot of people looking at it. Is that job done? No, it is not. Get the most out of it, take a close of the face, maybe it is a statue of an incredibly famous person, and take a picture of the sign? I shoot about 20-30 different images from just one statue.

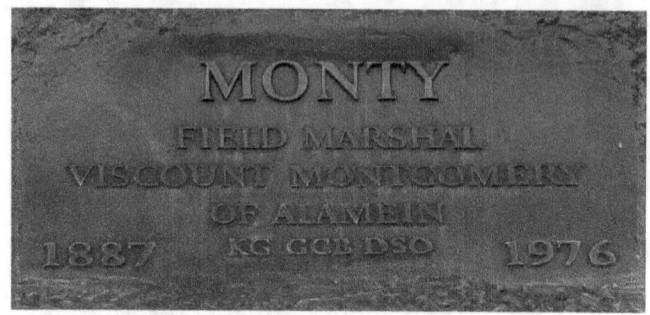

Look at the next three images. you could easily get another 20-30 images from this one statue of a famous general, walking around shooting at different angles, different lightning and so on.

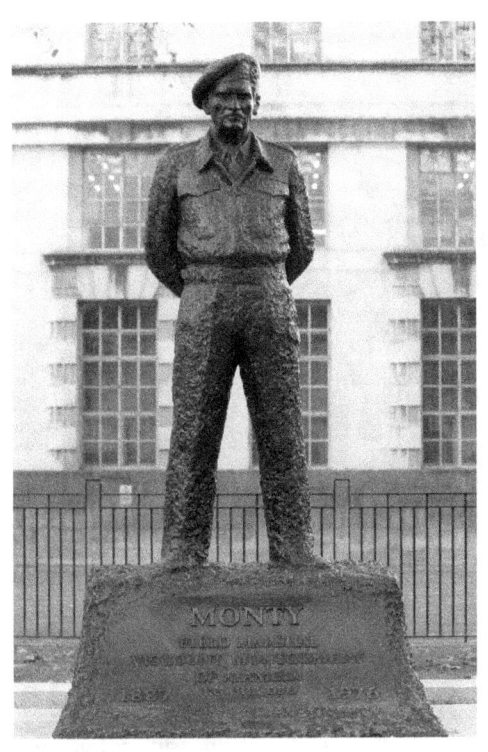

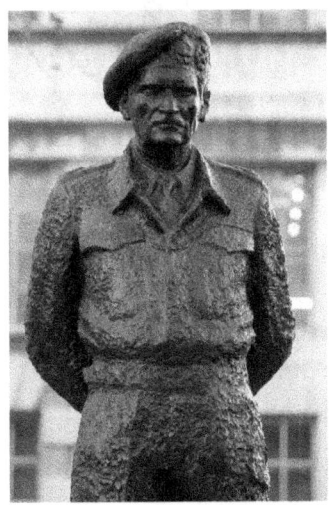

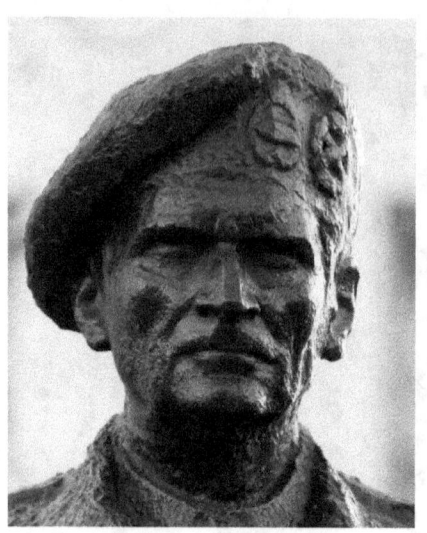

Busy shops and marketplaces, do wide general views but also do close ups people hands reaching for some fruit on a market stall. Fruit and vegetables on sale on a stall, the list is endless.

Classic architecture, like beautiful churches are particularly good, wide shots, and then close ups of the doorways, building structure. You can take pictures of brickwork and submit them as backgrounds! While you are there, there could be some lovely flowers and flower beds. People looking at the flowers. Try to involve people as much as possible, these are great editorial images and are used all the time for travel blogs and so on.

Travel images are popular, so on your next trip try to take as many shots as possible with people walking, leisure activities. Health and fitness are another big one, the world is crazy now for healthy living and fitness, exploit this as much as you can, close up shots of people eating healthy and do not forget unhealthy food! Eating a big bag of chips! At home you can do 1000's of images on your kitchen table, try to use natural light, showing all types of topical food, yogurts, salads on plates, do as many combinations as you can, close ups with hands in, knife and fork and nice angled shots.

Sports activities, people kicking a ball around in a local field, playing on the beach with a beach ball, do wide and trendy close shots, these are great editorial pictures.
The possibilities are literally endless.

Now I will give you a great **Top Tip** to get three times as many pictures from one set. When you do a set of pictures of say market scene with people, eating drinking, shopping and so on. Or any set of pictures really. Once you have edited them already for uploading you may end up with around 30-40 pictures. Now re- edited them! Crop wide shots in tighter. Crop tight shots even tighter! The photographic equipment we use these days can produce very high-quality images with large files sizes that can easily be re-cropped and will still be perfectly usable.

You can with a bit of thought and cropping turn one set of pictures from one shoot into another compete set which you can then submit to another library.
It is so easy; you are getting double the images from one set. But it gets better, now look through all your images the first edit and the cropped edit again and pick shots that you think will look nice in Black and White (Monochrome) I do this on every shoot and get another 30 percent of images again!
Monochrome images are extremely popular, and photographers miss this simple way to enlarge their portfolio from the same images! Remember though when you are captioning the images for submitting especially for editorial use to add in the description field that the image has been digitally altered to monochrome, like this in brackets (Image digitally altered to monochrome) With these two further tips you will be surprised how many more images you can create, I literally spent months going through my old library of images double cropping them and changes them to monochrome!

TOP TIP! With creative editing and using monochrome you can turn 30 images into 90! From one shoot. Convert you best images to monochrome and remember to double edited them!

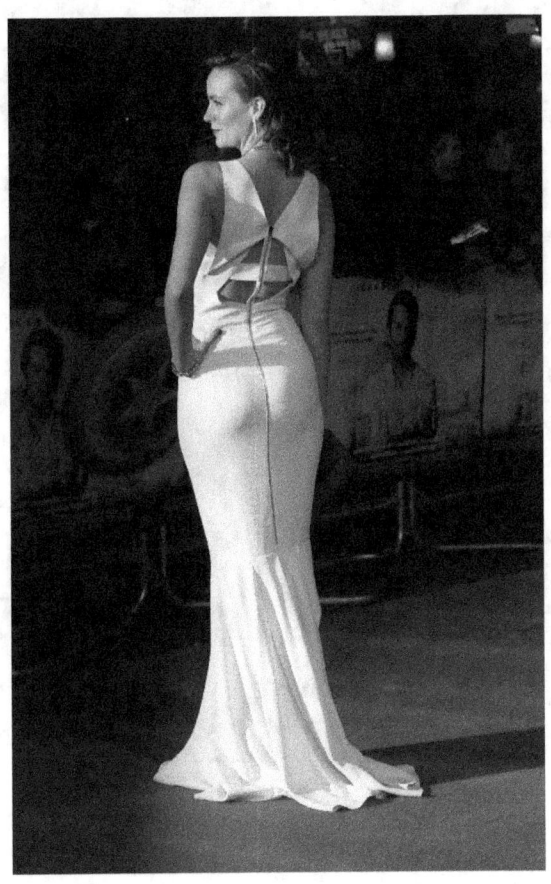

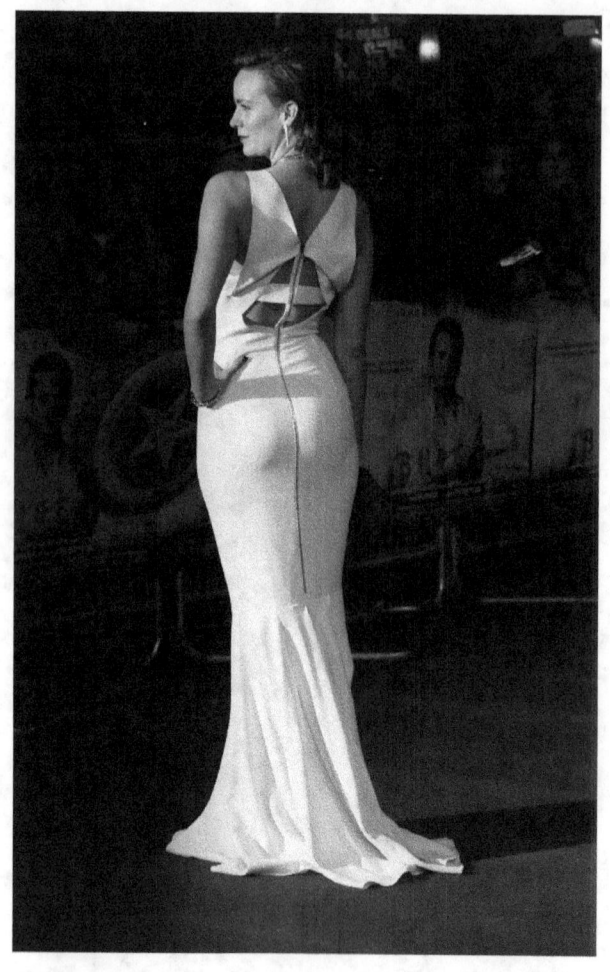

The point I am trying to make here is you must get
the absolute most from everything you can, I turned

a parked supercar in the street into about 75 images easily. Great editorial stock. And I was just walking around.

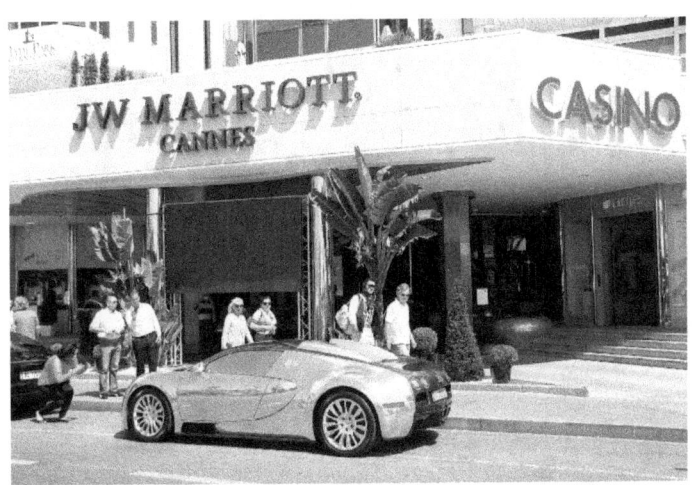

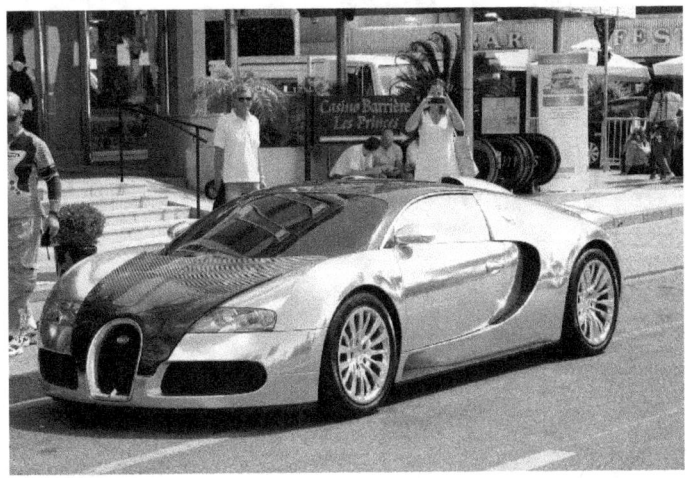

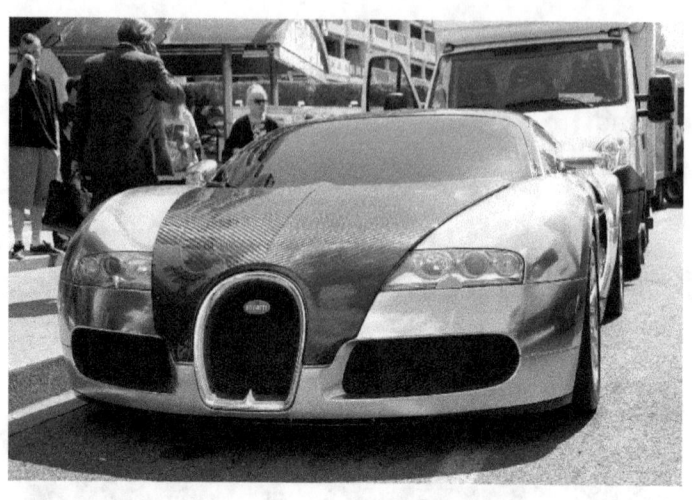

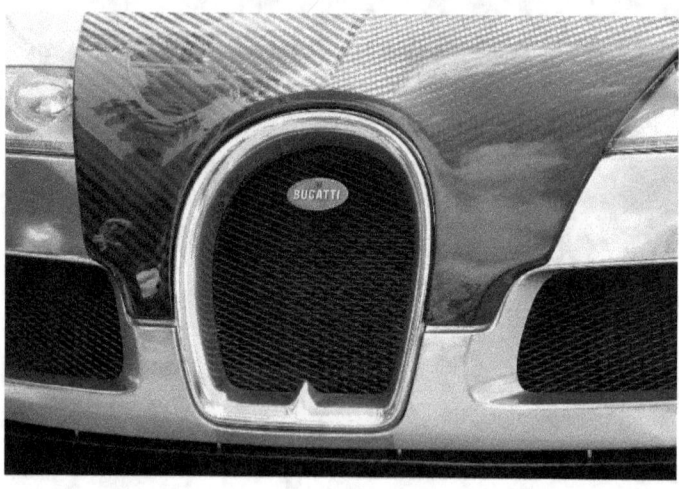

4 Where to send?

Image libraries explained

There are many companies out there to start sending images to in the stock photography market, just type stock images or Micro stock and your search engine will find plenty. I am going to recommend a couple and give you my reasons why I recommend them.

But first let us talk about what the difference is between a company selling Micro stock images and standard images. So, the standard way to sell an image online would be roughly like this: Your images would be found by a picture buyer, that buyer would select the type of use they intend for the image. Let us say for arguments sake they wanted a picture of someone typing on a keyboard for a book they are writing. The company holding your image would have a set price system to licence your picture for the use that the person buying the image would have to pay. So, in a nutshell, they download the image, pay the fee which could be something like £50, for use in their book for up to how many printed copies they said would be printed and maybe online use as well. That is all fine the agency gets £50 and pay you your percentage which is usually around 50% so you would get a nice £25.

Now micro stock agencies work differently, they hold huge amounts of images, but instead of charging a one-off fee for the use of an image their business model works differently, they charge a fixed subscription for many image downloads, say £200 per month and with that you can download 100 images for example. Now do not be put off by that because even after the sales are broken down to each contributor which means you might only get 25p per download or images purchased, they sell absolutely huge amounts!

So, once you have built up a large library of good quality images you will notice all those small download fees start to add up.

I have images with several libraries, and I tend to choose what pictures I upload to certain companies depending on what I think will sell best.

The other thing to point out with Micro Stock companies is that although they offer large quantity of images for relatively small amounts the licence, they issue for the use of those images can be quite limiting for the buyer. Most use is online for instance and no printed format.

So, you now have an idea of what the basic two types of image library companies are available to you.

I would suggest the best place to start is to Google the top 10 and have a look through them, looking at the different formats that they offer.

Two that I would highly recommend are **"Alamy"** A particularly good stock library that sells licences as per use of the image.

The other is **"Shutterstock"**
A massive micro stock company, a giant in this field and a major player when it comes to micro stock. Now both these companies have extremely strict submission guidelines, to do with image file sizes and quality. Please read through there help guilds before joining and take you time to submit your first images. Uploading images is very straight forward, they both has upload systems on their website, but you can FTP as well for larger quantities.
Good thing with Alamy is that you upload your images, then they go through their quality review process which can take about three to four days for stock. Then if they pass you can keyword and caption them within the Alamy platform which is excellent and easy to use.

This is different to Shutterstock; with them you must caption and keyword the images correctly before they go for the approval process. This to me is not so good for new photographers starting out, because it is a bit sole destroying to keyword, caption 50 images only to have load not approved. Once you get experience though rejections will get less. I just like the Alamy way that they approve the images first then you can do all the other stuff required to get them online for sale. Just seems a better way to me.

Once you have started uploading and have got your first images approved you will be on your way. Do not get dishearten if you have images rejected to start with, it is just a learning process so go on the forums and look for advice on them.

How to speed up your workflow?

Once you have started uploading and got some images approved you will be well on your way, next thing to do is to make your life as easy as possible with "Key wording" You will come to this once your first images are approved, each image that is uploaded will need to be key worded so that buyers can search and find your images with the keywords that they search with. I cannot emphasise enough that key wording is crucial! You need to put detailed keywords to match your images. But do not just spam out your key wording by adding 100s of words that do not accurately describe your images. Stock agencies are clamping down on this now.

TOP TIP put phrases! Like "Working at my desk" for images that show a laptop and mouse. "Workstation and mouse" rather than just separate words like

"Laptop" "Mouse "try to link what is in the images together. "Working from home "for instance.

There are loads of editing software out on the market that will have IPTC template settings that you can add text, keywords, copyright and contact info to which can then be applied to each image. This way once the image is uploaded to your chosen image library it should be ready for captioning with all the fields that you have pre-loaded with your editing software intact.

Now I am going to recommend a piece of software that I have used for many years called "Photo mechanic" it is ridiculously cheap about £50 or so. I can honestly say it is one of the best easiest to use and will speed up your workflow. I am not going to go into all its functions in too much depth, the best way is to download the trial version which at the time of going to press I believe is still available. But one feature that I like that I will mention is this. Once you have downloaded your memory card to your laptop or PC you can open this image folder in **"Photo Mechanic",** it will show all the images in that folder. You can very quickly look through the images and mark with one simple click your best images, this is called tagging the images. Once you have done this you simply click show all tagged images and the workspace will then show only the files you have tagged which should be your best images from that shoot. So, you can see its amazingly fast and nice way to quickly look through your images selecting the best ones. It does have loads of other features, even minor image adjustments.

File FTP transfer which is handy for up loading images direct to your chosen stock companies. I really can say its money well spent and unless you want to go into heavy image manipulation then its' probably all you will ever need. If you do want to learn about image manipulation and layers and so, then you will need something like PS (Photoshop) to mention just one of the many available.

What computer skills do I need?

Most people have some good computer skills and knowledge especially with the increased use of Smartphones and tablets. Therefore, you do not need to worry too much about if you will have the right skills to process all these images you will be taking. Things you will need to learn how to do will be re-sizing of your images to fit in with the requirements of the image libraries that you have chosen to submit to. Also captioning the images with the IPTC templates. Basic image manipulation is very straight forward, using tools such as curves, brightness, and basic colour adjustments will be straightforward and easy to use. If you decided to use Photo Mechanic, it does come with some basic image tools as described in the previous section. However later you may start to want to enhance your stock images to improve sales, editorial images should not be edited too much, only basic adjust should are allowed as the image should only be used as part of an information or news item. But for general stock images of lovely views, Landscapes, modelling sets and so on, you can really go to town with enhancing your images. Once you get to this stage you will probably want to use something like P.S. (Photoshop) or similar. These types of software are immensely powerful and offer absolutely loads of image manipulation. Now there are plenty of tutorials on YouTube to get you started with them and you will be surprized how quickly you can get familiar with the software.

What is the advantaged in having expensive equipment?

Good question and one I get asked a lot, people say "well I can never make any money out of photography because I don't have all the pro gear!" Wrong, as I said before you can even start doing stock photography with a reasonable mobile phone, but there are limitations. I will go onto using a mobile phone in the next section. Now with digital equipment you can purchase for relatively small amount of money, say £200- 300 dollars a good used DSLR or compact type mirrorless camera. Even with a basic kit lens. So, I am going to try and give some examples of the pros and cons and the disadvantage you may come across with the lower priced equipment compared to the higher priced professional equipment including the lens.

First a little bit about what I believe is the most important part of your photography equipment, the lens. I would rather have a slow old camera body with a good quality lens then an expensive camera body with a cheap lens, now I will try to explain why. In the end of the day any image you capture is obtained by going through the lens. So, it stands to reason that this is an important part of your kit. With some of the cheaper compact cameras they do have a fixed lens that you cannot change. They may have what would seem a good range, something like 17mm – 200mm which sounds brilliant and yes, it is a huge focal range. But what you will find is that images taken at every extremity of the lens, i.e., 17mm as wide as it will go, or at the other end of the scale 200mm so zoomed right in, you will find that the quality will deteriorate steeply.

Also, these types of lenses are noticeably light hungry, and they only stop down to sometimes f5.6 at the widest part of the range. Which means you need reasonable amount of light available and which in turn gives you less flexibly. Usually build quality, weather proofing will also come into it. Now of course you cannot really compare a standard kit lens that cost £50 to something like the superb Canon 70 – 200mm mk2 IS f2.8 which costs around £2000 But I just wanted to point out that these factures do play a part in having the most flexibility when shooting. For instance, I used my Canon 70-200 when I did a close of the face on a statue, I think attempting that shot with a lower end quality lens I would not have got the sale that I did. So, quality of kit does play a part to some degree.

Regarding camera bodies, you can spend £300 and get a good DSLR, but what is the main difference between that and the latest Canon Mk 5? Costing £5K Well there are loads of things, but things that directly affect photography are for instance, when I talked about ISO settings. With equipment costing around 5k it will almost certainly have a full frame sensor and have far better image processing software. With this type of equipment, you can use much higher ISO settings like 2000 ISO and higher and get an exceptionally clean usable image. This will give you more flexibility when taking pictures. You can get much cheaper full frame equipment, please see the section discussing crop versus full frame, this which might be worth considering.

Another big advantage in more expensive equipment is the speed at which the camera can shoot frames or pictures, high end equipment can shoot extremely fast up to 14 frames per second, now for general stock images this really is not important, but if you want to enter the world of sports photography or press work then really this will play a big part. Cheaper lower end equipment will normally shoot at around 5 frames per second or less. But again, for standard stock images this will do perfectly fine as you do not need to shoot fast and hundreds of frames! These are just a few samples of why more expensive equipment will give you more flexibly. I personally would spend as much as possible on your lens as this is money well spent and once you have a good selection of high-quality lens and provided you stay with the same manufacture and lens mount you can upgrade your camera body later. I keep my lenses for years and years and hardly ever change them.

So, when you are making a start or buying any new equipment think about these things and your long-term goals. It will save you money in the long run. You will never go wrong buying quality lenses for sure.

5 What can you buy for £200!

If you are buying a camera from scratch, you will be surprized what you can get for £200-300, I would go for a good quality second-hand model. Look on eBay or social media sites, I picked up a lovely second-hand Canon 7D Mk1 for £200 on eBay, mint condition in the box, it was about 4-5 five years old, A real bargain, when this model was first released, I purchased one and paid £1200 for it! so a few years down the line and I got one at a fraction of the price. It is a great camera 12mp, fast, excellent quality and build. Not a full frame sensor but still particularly good. Look for something that has a low shutter count or one that has been used by a video blogger, they tend to be in surprisingly good condition.

Full Frame or Crop sensor?

The sensor on your camera is the part that captures the image, there are a quite a few different types and formats and I am going to give a brief explanation on what the main differences are. Crop sensor cameras tend to be more compact, sometimes mirrorless, sometimes DSLR, (Digital Single Lens Reflex) virtually all compact cameras have what is called a crop sensor. So, what is meant by "crop" Well originally back in the days of film most SLR cameras (Single Lens Reflex) would use a 35mm film. Now recent years more Full frame digital sensors have come on the market, they have been around for a long time, but they were much more expensive, now they have come down in price considerable. A full frame digital sensor is basically the same size as a single frame on an original 35mm film. Therefore, they have mirrored this size and format in digital format calling a full frame. A crop sensor is a small version of a full frame, Crop factures can vary from 1.2 to 1.6

So, what are the advantages of a full frame sensor and what does the crop effect on crop sensors do?. If you are using a crop sensor the cropping factor will be the crop, say 1.6 x the focal length of your lens attached. So, for instance if you had a standard 50mm lens attached to a crop sensor camera with a crop facture of 1.6 the actual focal length of the lens would be multiplied by 1.6 thus giving you focal length lens of 80mm. So, in effect the lens would be working as an 80mm lens rather than its true focal length size of 50mm. If you attach a standard 50mm lens to a full frame censor it word wok as a 50mm lens just like it did on a standard 35mm film camera. Now most manufactures develop lenses that are design specifically for their crop sensor equipment.

So, benefits and disadvantages. This is a widely debated subject with vary views. But the straightforward facts are that a full frame sensor will have distinct advantages over a crop sensor in certain conditions and areas. However, in certain conditions there really is no advantage at all. Biggest advantage is being able to shoot image on much higher ISO settings, this is because the sensor is physical bigger and therefore it captures the image at better quality because the actual pixels that make it up are spaced more apart in most cases. Being able to raise your ISO with no loss of quality is real big bonus especially for shooting stock image in low light conditions. Being able to raise the ISO to levels like 2000 or 3000 and still get a clean nice image is useful for sports photographers for example, by having the facility to raise your ISO up will give you the opportunity in turn to shoot at higher shutter speeds for instance which for sports photography is a real bonus as they are normally amazingly fast-moving subjects. Also, because the quality of a full frame is usually better if you were required to make large prints from you images you could print then exceptionally large indeed without any loss of quality. But this really is not a factor for virtually everything we shoot is online now and pretty much limits the size to relatively small scales.

Disadvantages for a full frame sensor, well one being if you clean your own sensor like I do, it tends to be a bit harder to accomplish, however there not too many people around that clean their own sensors, smaller crop sensor are a lot easier to clean. Please note I do not recommend you attempt to clean your sensor yourself; I am very experienced with this type of thing, so it comes easy to me. If you do not know what you are doing you can damage the sensor very easily then you are looking at an awfully expensive repair bill. So, do not attempt it unless you really feel you want to. Of course, full frame cameras tend to be more expensive, although in recent years the price has come down a lot. Another thing to consider is the crop factor that you are losing, it is quite handy sometimes to have a crop facture. I had a Canon 7D with a crop factor of 1.6, this was very handy for a particular job I was doing where the subject was a long way off, I have a 300mm lens and a 2x convertor, put these all on the camera gave me an actual lens focal length of 960mm! Imagine the cost of a lens at that focal length! So, a crop sensor really did me a big favour especially as the job I was doing was a one off. So, it is not like a really wanted to have 1000mm lens sittings around for one job a year.

Stock pictures with a mobile phone?

Can you do stock photography with a mobile phone? Yes, you can, and it is certainly a good way to get started! I have taken plenty of stock pictures with my mobile phone and sold plenty as well.

There are now actually companies and sites that specialise in mobile phone images for sale, Alamy have an App called "Stockimo" you can take a picture and upload it directly to their site, you do not even need a laptop or PC. Most mobile phones now have image editing as well, or there are some good apps that you can download for basic editing.
The truth is you can start with a mobile phone, and it is a very covenant way to get started, and why not, everyone carries a mobile around with them these days, so the benefits are you always have it with you. And why not get started? like I mentioned at the start of this book the sooner you start the better, I cannot emphasise this enough, building an image library takes time, but you have nothing to lose it can only grow and so can the income from it. Imaged if you started this 5 years ago, how many images would you have out online? 5000! You might be making £250 a month from them. How bad it that? You cannot go wrong, now a mobile phone will be limiting, do not get me wrong I'm not saying that its perfect, far from it, but it's a start.
Tips for pictures not to bother with are the following, Low light pictures, night-time pictures,

mobile phone use very tiny lenses, they can only take in so much light, although the pixel count might sound impressive for the camera on the phone like 12 million pixels, it really means nothing, as however good the sensor might be and the processing power of the phone, in the end of the day the image captured is by a tiny lens, end of story. So, do not waste too much time attempting to take good stock images in low light conditions, even with a tripod because they will have limited use and you will be only able to submit them to a few agencies.

Use your mobile phone as a flexible extremely portable tool and get the most from it by using it when in good lighting conditions.

The good thing about them is they are so small you can use them to get some great trendy looking pictures at extreme angles and different from even a small compact camera. Take pictures from low down, ground level or high up, where you would not normally attempt to take a picture.

6 Wedding Photography

Tips and brief guide

First, lets me please emphasize that you should not attempt to shoot a wedding until you have been fully trained by an expert. I train photographers to shoot weddings, the process I use is very comprehensive, the student will attend 3-4 weddings as a second photographer and then I will shadow them on 1 – 2 full weddings until they are confident in their ability. But I have decided to give a few tips and a brief guide here as you may wish to progress to this excellent career or even have it as an extra income.

So, a simple system that will never let you down. It seems obvious but you will need to have double or spare everything equipment wise. I would never attempt to photograph a wedding without a complete double kit. Now do not forget the simplest things like having plenty of memory cards.

Top Tip
And talking of memory cards get into the habit of changing your memory card after shooting around 100 images. That way if you do have a problem with a particular memory card you would not lose an entire wedding shoot. So, I just changed my card every 100 shots or so as a precaution.

I have photographed over 2000 or more weddings throughout my career, in that time I have never had a card failure. And remember I started out photographing weddings using film! So, try and imagine how nerve racking that was. If for any reason you do get a card failure, do not panic there are plenty of card recovery software companies around that in virtually all circumstance hopefully will be able to recover your images or at least some of them.

So spare equipment and plenty of memory cards is a must. Something else that I do which is always a good idea, if you are travelling by your own transport to the wedding venue, which probably will be most of you. Take along a spare set of cloths, I always take two white shirts with me. Sounds silly but you could easily stop off for a coffee or something to eat just before the wedding and spill a drink down your shirt! Try and imagine, with maybe only an hour to go to the wedding and your shirt or blouse has a massive coffee stain right down the front! Trust me it could happen, and I am sure it has, but never too me fortunately, so be prepared in full.

I always make a note of a local taxi company near by the venue in case of a break down. That way if you were to have the miss fortune to break down you could just leave your car where it is, call a taxi and at least then you will be sure to make it to the venue in time to photograph the wedding, which is the priority and get your car recovered later.

Even something like a flat tyre could delay you and you just cannot risk anything like that because it is someone's wedding, A once in a lifetime event. Not really something you can miss just because you could not arrive on time. So, allow plenty of time! I plain to arrive at the wedding venue at least one hour before I am due to start working. For two reasons, one in case of transport problems, the other if you have not done a pre - venue walk around, it gives you plenty of time to have a good look around and check out nice places where you will be shooting your groups shots and so on.

Speak to the vicar and find out what's allowed photography wise during the ceremony, some places for instance do not allow any use of flash at all in the church if it is a church wedding. But really the only time you might need flash is during the signing of the register shots for instance. It is not like you would use flash during the ceremony anyway.

So, you have come fully prepared and in plenty of time. That is a good start because the last thing you want is any stress just before you are about to photograph someone special day.

Regarding types if pictures to take. Now I can tell you nowadays everyone likes a good mix of informal candid type pictures and then the set standard posed pictures. I am going to explain a bit about these types of images now. When have your initial meeting with the prospective bride and groom that are plaining a wedding, a high percentage will say that they want all informal candid type shots. Well, the truth is they really do want those because they look cool and trendy but without a shadow of a doubt, they will also want all those classic set posed pictures as well. So, what are the classic set posed pictures that you take at a wedding.

Well, we have all been to weddings so hopefully you will have an idea. But lets us go through some of the essentials. Bride arriving with father or whoever is giving her away. I always do a nice setup posed shot of them. Best thing to do is a nice shot of the bride sitting in the car before she gets out, try to get her holding her bouquet of flowers nice and close so you can see them. It is not always easy as there is not normally much room, but you will be surprised how popular this shot is. Then do a nice shot of her with her father or whoever is giving her away, posed standing together before they go into the venue.

Now during the wedding, itself you need to be sure what the couple want, the essential pictures are putting the rings on and the first kiss for instance. During the actual ceremony I do not like to take to many shots and try to stay at the back of the venue normally a church only coming down to the front for the putting the rings on part or the ceremony and the first kiss.

I personally think a photographer crowding around to close to the front is very off putting for the bride and groom, who will be nervous enough anyway. During this part of the proceedings, it is normally deadly silent and the sound of a camera clicking during the actual words being spoken is I think just too intrusive. We need to remember that this is an absolute special day and although you do need to do your job, I do not think you need to intrude too much during this part. It is a special and most intimate part of the ceremony, in my opinion. Something that should be treasured and not spoiled by some over enthusiastic photographer clambering around trying to get more pictures. The truth is there are only so many shots you can really get during the actual ceremony, and they will not be all that interesting really. Just the couple standing there repeating the words! While spoil that moment for them. But please do speak with the couple and ask them what they think, to be sure you take the shots that want, it's their money at the end of the day.

Then we come to the signing of the register if they are having that part of the ceremony. I always do a nice set picture of the couple signing. What I do here is just let them sign as they are directed to by whoever is taking the ceremony, you can take a few candid shots while this takes place. Then after all the official signing has been done, I will do a set up shot of the couple pretending to sign, sounds silly but it works well. Just ask the bride to hold the pen and have the registrar's book laid out in front of them, so its looks like they are signing, then just get them to look up, smile and that your picture. One nice touch is to place the bride's bouquet on the table just in front of them, just adds to the picture with a nice bit of colour.

After the ceremony and when they are coming out of the venue stop them in the doorway and get a nice shot of them kissing in the doorway, it is a simple shot that takes a second but looks great and they will thank you for it. Once they come out, I will do a few shots of the couple together, but I will have them placed in position for where I would be doing my group shots. This way while you are doing some of the happy couple it will give time for the guests to come out of the venue and gather around. After that I will shoot the formal groups shots. I ways do this straight away because people will start to do their own little groups shots anyway so better to do all the formal shots, like with mum and dad, uncle bob and so. Don't' restrict what you do ask the couple if they want any shots with certain members of their family, is there big day so make sure you get every they will want, they may have guests coming from all around the world so a do some nice posed up shots for them. Once that all done then the real great pictures can come. I them stand back and let the happy couple mix with all their friends and relatives and get as much candid reportage style pictures as I can.

They love these images of them interacting with family and friends. And do not forget to take plenty of the guest as like aunt Ethel and Uncle Bob having laugh. I absolutely love shooting weddings; everyone is so happy all; smiles and enjoying them self and you find if you just walk around with a good zoom lens on you can get some stunning stuff. I use my 70-200 f2.8 for this, it is basally perfect just enough zoom to get close ups when need to, so you can keep your distance and just wonder around. People soon forget you are there and that is when the absolute best pictures will come. Now while talking about style of pictures, I can give you a good tip, when presenting you portfolio to a perspective couple or on your galleries online. Put plenty and I mean plenty of candid reportage style images! And plenty in monochrome. These images are so poplar they will get you the bookings. Simple rule, Candid gets the bookings, but you still need the posed pictures at the end of the day because everyone will want them. If you are offering on-line sales or providing prints, I guarantee every pose set picture you take, all; the groups shots and pose set images will sell! Everyone will be purchased by guests and friends. It is just funny really all the couples say oh we really want candid style images, but I guarantee they will want the classic set images as well.

Once you have done plenty of candid material you can then do some nice one on one posed portraits with the bride and groom.

Some more classic shots that will really be expected. Confetti shots, I always do this after I have got every else that I wanted of the bride and groom, it works well to set up a confetti shot at the end before they set of to the reception venue, if it is being held at a different location to the actual wedding venue. If it is in the same venue, then just do the confetti shot before they go into the reception? Gather all the guests around and set up the shot, do a count down and everyone will throw their confetti and a laugh, and it will make great pictures.

During the evening there are only a couple of essential pictures that you need. You can do some nice candid shots of the speeches. Then the cutting of the cake, again with this I will do a set up posed picture with the bride and groom pretending to cut the cake. Then just take a few candid shots as they do it for real in front of the guests. Last pictures of what would be an exceptionally long day is the first dance, then I would be on my way, exhausted. All that is left then, is the next day to edit all the material. Remember when you edit to convert lots of images to monochrome, people love black and white images.

7 Press, News and celebrity work

How to start, where to start?

Press, News and Celebrity work. It is daunting knowing where to start with this one. A lot will be dependent on where you are located and what is available. But with a little bit of thought you might be able to add this to your forte. Celebrity pictures are great stock pictures, especially of iconic people. They also have a direct and instant sale value, especially if there is a particular interest in that person at that time.

But I am going to start with news photography. Once you have become confident of your skills you could approach your local newspaper and ask if they ever need anything covered on a freelance basis, if they would give you some jobs to cover that are of local interest. They might be interested you never know. I was approached by my local free newspaper and asked if I could cover some odd assignments for them, many years ago. It was straight forward and easy stuff to cover, they did a section on new-born babies in the area so they would send me along to the local hospital to do a few portraits of parents and their new-born baby. Sometimes they would send me to a local event or the opening of a new shop with a special interest, stuff like that straight forwarded.

Newspapers are struggling now as it is a dimensioning market. They tend to have one or two permanent staff photographers. But with holidays and sickness they can often get caught out and need freelancers to step in. This could be your opportunity. Contact your local newspaper and get the contact details of their assignment's manager, send him a nice email with links to some of you best images or portfolio. Give them your availability and contact details. But try to be reliable, it is no good saying that you are availably 24/7 when in fact you are not. Think about what days or hours you defiantly will be free. These opportunities come rarely but you will find that if they need someone, they will contact you, but it could be short notice, so do not expect days of notice to do a job for them. This will come later if they start using you consistently, then they will plain and offer you shifts in advance. Initially it is likely they could call you first thing in the morning as someone has called in sick and they have 3 jobs that need to be covered. So, you will get a 7.30am call asking if you can work for them today. It is important to be able to say "yes sure no problem" because that is what they as want to hear, and this is your chance to get your foot in the door. You might only get one chance so make sure you take it. The other way they work with someone new is they will assign you a couple of jobs with plenty of notice just to see how reliable you are and what your work is like. If you are lucky and do get the opportunity, it is a great way to expand your portfolio.

Now how to get into the celebrity and red carpet or photography? This is really dependant on where you live. It is all well, and good saying yes go out try to take pictures of celebrities to get you started, but that is not much good if you live in the middle of nowhere! So, I am not going to mislead you and pretend that it will be easy. However, you might have a large town or preferably a city nearby that you could or maybe your work takes you to on occasions. If you are lucky maybe you work in a large city. In which case you can make a start in your spare time.

So where to start. There are plenty of celebrity news type agencies online that cover this type of stuff worldwide. Again, depending on where you live and what is going on will determine the quickest route to start getting into this field. I would start by doing some research on what media outlets you have that will be available to you. Once you have established that there are some around, like a radio station or broadcasting company you then will possibly have some potential to get some celebrity pictures in one form or another. Because if you have absolutely nothing around you that you could possibly be shooting and unless you are prepared to travel where things are going on then, there is really no point.

If you have a large city that is within easy reach, or your work commitments take you to one. Then I would approach an agency straight away. Could be that they have plenty of freelance work based on commission available and this is a great way to get started. If they are a good agency, they will have tips and events that they can send you too straight away. I found that doing research myself really pays off. Look for a radio or television broadcasting company and find out where they do there broadcasting from. You can easily look through the schedules and see what guests they may be interviewing on the shows. Then look at the venues and see if you could get some paparazzi style pictures, celebrities or presenters seen arriving or leaving. If you can this is a great way to get involved with a big photo agency as they will always be interested in these types of images. Look for local and international politicians as well. They often visit radio and television locations for interviews on in the news events and items. This really is a great way to get started and again get your foot in the door with a top world class agency. Then you can hopefully start to be assigned red carpet and events that they need covered. You never know maybe you will make it to the Cannes Film festival one day! I really hope you do.

Sports photography, I have not really done too much sports photography, just a few football games and a bit of celebrity sporting events. But you can apply the same principles, find out about matches being held, even minor league games of sporting events can be a good way to expand your portfolio and open doors to getting into media type work. The only thing to think about is that you really will need good photographic equipment for fast action sports events. But you will be surprised what can be achieved with entry level gear provided you shoot clever. Keep your settings on file sizes small on your camera this will help the processing speed of your equipment and will help to shoot faster frames which will be needed for sports. If your lens is not the greatest set your ISO up higher than normal as quality is not such as an issue. Remember to turn down you image noise reduction settings to low. As this setting could slow your camera down if it is an entry level one. Keep your shutter speed high to freeze the action.

One tip for and sports involving a ball like Soccer, Rugby, American football, baseball. Try to get shots where the ball is in the frame! No one wants to see a picture of a football striker making a goal shooting shot without the ball in the frame. Simple but easy to forget. Baseball, the picture just about to strike the ball. Catcher jumping for the ball but with the ball in the frame. This is important for soccer or football. With motorsport try using the panning technic (see Panning) to give your pictures a sense of speed rather than just a static picture of a race car on the track, the only time that looks good is when they crash! If you are luckily enough to have a reasonable motorsport venue within easy reach, try approaching the media and press department and see if they will let you come down track side during practice session to get some experience. You can get some good stock pictures as well while you are there.

If you do get the chance to attend any celebrity photocalls or events, remember to shoot as much as possible, small details go a long way with impressing pictures desks and assignments managers. Do tight crops showing hair, jewellery and handbag details.

8 Architecture:

The good the bad and the ugly!

Beautiful architecture images can sell well in stock photography, but there are a few pitfalls and I want to touch on a few subjects. What makes a good architectural image? When to shoot and when not to. Lighting this is without any doubt the most important part of good architecture images. I have been to location to shoot interesting building and walk away without taking a picture, why? Because the light was not right. You cannot force a picture that is just simply not there. You can however why you are there assess if the light will be better at certain times of the day, like early morning, midday or evening when the sun is in different position and lighting the building totally differently at that time. Now why is this important, have a look at the images that show good and bad lighting?

Poor light, heavy shadows on one side of the telephone boxes.

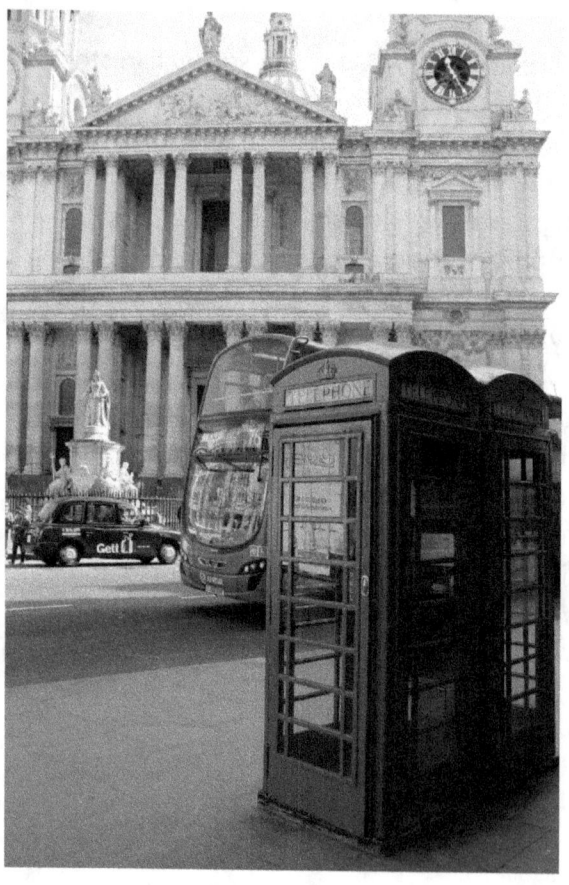

Next even worse! Why would anyone want to use or buy this image!

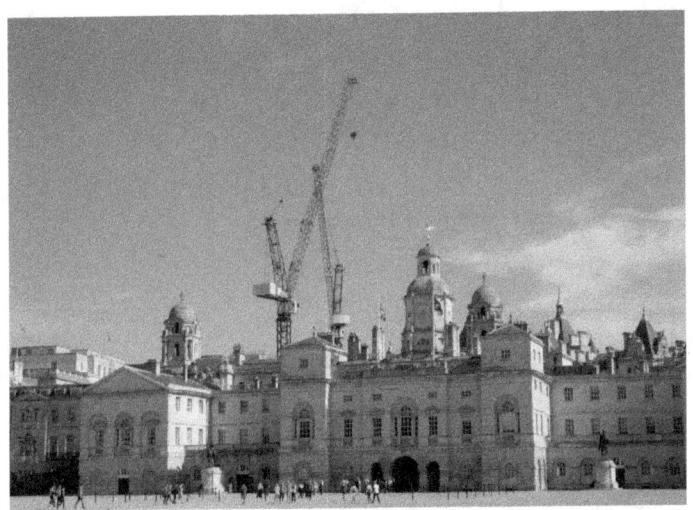

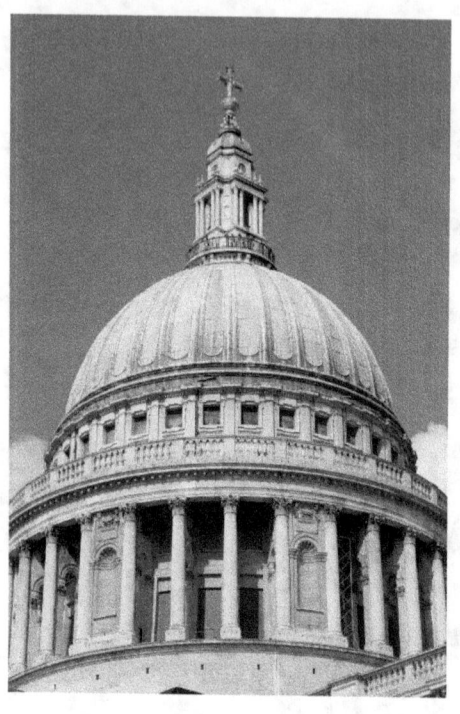

Much more evenly lit, you can see every detail of the building, no dark areas. You will find that with some architecture that you just cannot ever get a good evenly lit image, it does happen. If that is the case think about the possibilities of shooting a totally different image, plain maybe a night shoot if the building is nicely lit up at night, or maybe a trendy daybreak or a sunset type of image. Normally you can find a way to get something with a bit of plaining and thought.

9 Tips on using flash Photography

Using flash can be very troublesome for new photographers even experienced ones! So, for this section I will be giving you some useful tips and try to explain some fundamentals.

Most people buy what is called a dedicated flash gun which is almost certainly manufactured by the same company of their camera equipment. Stand to reason that in theory this should make using a flashgun easier. Obviously, I can just go through and tell you about every combination of make, model and how that work together. But there are a few things that are going to be familiar with most types and models. They might have settings that are called something different, but they will have similar usages.

Ok so once you have your flash connected you will probably have some settings on it like TTL or ETTL stuff like that. These will be the settings for synchronizing the flash with the camera. By default, the camera will probably set the shutter speed to 1/160sec or possibly 1/200sec this is the standard settings for the shutter to correctly synchronize with the flash when it fires. One thing that does tend to happen when the flash is set in this mode is that it tends to give out too much light causing your images to washout and be over exposed. This will vary depending on what you are shooting. One simple tip to reduce the output of the flash while keeping it in fully auto mode is to look for the exposure compensation setting on the flash gun. Scroll through the menus and looks for something that says exposure compensator + or – once you find this select it and take it down or minus it by one or half a stop. This will reduce the output but keep the flashgun in sync with the camera when it fires. Do a bit of trial and error and you will soon find the best setting.

TOP TIP,

If you want to add fill in flash using your flashgun during the day or in good light this is the easiest way. Rather than trying to set it up on fully manual which you can do, what I do is leave it on auto but adjust the exposure compensator right down which will normally be about 3 stops. You will find that this works perfect as a fill in setting on most flash guns. If you do want to use your flash gun as fill in but on totally manual, just set it 3 stops down from the correct exposure and that should be about right.

Catch Flash:

What is it and how to do it!

Catch flash, what is it how to do it. I will explain, first though you can only get a catch flash type image if there are lots of photographers and loads of flashes going off at the same time. So, for this reason you can only really attempt it during what are called photo calls with all the press guys working. Or events like film premieres again when there is a press pack and lots of camera flashes will be going off at the same time.

So how does it work and how can you achieve this masterpiece of photography and I do not say that lightly because the images you can get with catch flash look stunning.
The mechanics of it are simple enough. Normally you would have your flashgun set to synchronise with your camera to flash or send its output at the correct time and quantity to light the area or person to get a correctly exposed picture.

Your equipment might be set up something like, shutter speed at 1/200sec aperture at say f5.6 or f8 ISO around 200. Now to get a catch flash image, you will take your pictures at the same time as all the others in the photographer's pen or, but set your camera up like this, turn your flash gun off! Shutter speed set low, like 1/60sec or 1/80sec, F stop around the f8 ISO unchanged. You also want your camera to shoot as fast as possible so set the frame speed to maximum it will go. Because in order to get a catch flash image you will be relying on capturing someone else's flash when it goes off during the photocall. This is literally what you are hoping for.

So, set you camera up as describe and as soon as the shooting starts just hold the shutter button down and fire off as many frames as possible. You will need to hold your camera very, very steadily as you are shooting at an exceptionally low shutter speed so camera shack can be a real problem. You will find with a bit of luck and practice while you are shooting hopefully out of one of the frames your camera will pick up someone's else's flash, this will give you that studio lightening effect and created great images. Depending on the available light that is at the venue will affect greatly the pictures that you get. It takes a bit of practice and fine tuning of your settings again depending on the available light, the number of photographers that are present which effects how much other flashlight be being produced at the time. But it is worth the effect and the results are really stunning when done right.

Nice example of using the catch flash technic.

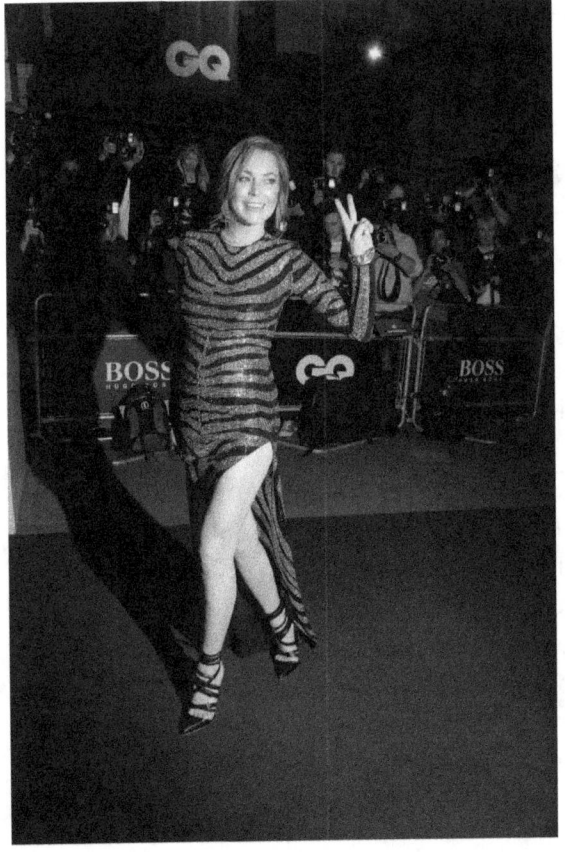

10 Videography

In this section I will discuss shooting video for stock. You might not be interested in shooting video at this stage, but latter on I hope you will as this is a particularly good growing market, and you can use the skills we have learnt together and implement them into video very easily. You will need to learn some new skills, like basic editing but do not be daunted by this, editing video clips is straight forward for stock purposes. Now advance video editing is really something else, but for stock clips only considerably basic editing like cut and snip are required. Most reasonable cameras come with video capabilities and mobiles phones certainly do. Although I must admit I have never attempted to shoot a clip for stock purposes on my mobile phone. Whether they will be good enough quality I am not sure. Probably in good light and with a particularly good mobile you can get away with it. But probably would not be too much trouble to try to submit and see if the clip would be accepted, I have just always used my camera.

Now one thing you will need is reasonable PC or laptop with plenty of memory and it should be quite high specifications. Video clips tend to be very large files and it can be a very slow process attempting to download and edit clips on a poor-quality computer. One thing you will notice is that most the captioning and key wording must be done once the clip is uploaded to the platform you are selling on.

Shutterstock do sell a large amount of video clips; I have several hundred on their platform. Pond5 is another one that I use. There are plenty of other platforms out there, but these are the two that I can recommend. Uploading is straight forward on both these platforms, waiting time to get your clips approved can vary a lot. So, what type of clips could you be submitting? Well, I have tried a few different types, video is not my main interest, but I have to say it is growing with me all the time. I have submitted a few general view type clips panning and doing some basic cut and join type editing. Sales are not bad considering the number of clips I have.

My best sellers seem to be wide shots and popular ones seems to be at night, for instance going to a press night and taking a wide shot of all the Press photographers taking pictures on the red carpet seems to be extremely popular I have sold one of these clips about 30 times. Look out for local events going on, anything that draws a crowd and get some nice general views crowds clapping and cheering that type of thing. Of course, if you do not have anything like this going on where you live then unfortunately it is not something that you can do. I would suggest maybe leisure activates might be a good place to start, perhaps doing some stuff around a local beach or seaside area. One subject that I have had absolutely no success with is doing a set video on things like a coffee machine making coffee or a printer printing out a form. To me I thought these might have some value. My clips are not particularly brilliant to it might be worth giving a few things around the house a try, you could do something like someone drawing the curtain to shield the sun out. Stuff like that, could be some demand for it. The other subject that I think could be a seller is clips of maybe farming or any farming activities, tractors going along ploughing a field this type of thing. Stuff related to food is normally good and of course anything related to health and fitness, so get you friend to jump on a fitness bicycle and do a clip of them. I think health has a lot of scope and future for good quality clips. One tip check the sound on your clips. If it is spoiled but someone shouting or something like that just remove it.

A lot of clips that I have sold have had no sound on them at all. It is extremely easy to remove it with some basic video editing software. I think when companies purchase video clips they are not as bothered about the sound as they probably use them for presentations, and they just overlay the clips with their own sound or music.

Clip's length does not need to be long, check with the company that you are submitting to but as a guild I think the longest is about 60 second, most my clips are around 30 seconds. Also, most companies require clips to be submitted in MP4 format, but again check their requirements to be sure.

TOP TIP

Be incredibly careful with the auto focus setting when shooting video clips. Depending on the camera settings, the auto-focus setting could result in your camera continuously jumping from one place to another in the image- especially if your camera has facial recognition software. You may therefore think you are recording a nice generic view of a seaside which will quickly be ruined when a person walks past within the camera focus range. This is because the auto-focus function can result in the camera focusing on the person walking past and starting to trace the person. This can then ruin the whole shoot of the recording. I, therefore, always set my focus on manual. Then the focus in normally homed in on something stationary in the image, like a building or another non-specific object. Video clips, in general, are useless if the focus is jumping around.

Another important thing to remember is that the camera must be kept stable. As you can imagine, this is because any movement in a video clip looks terrible. I would recommend always using a tripod or supporting yourself up against a wall set object as the camera's platform. If you are really stuck, I tend to stabilise the camera with two hands and push my arms into my chest for the extra stability. Luckily, the short video clips are roughly 60 seconds or so, meaning the uncomfortable posture does not need to be held for long. With practice, I am confident that you will be able to maintain the camera's stability and focus long enough to capture that perfect clip.

11 Thoughts going forward

I hope you have thoroughly enjoyed reading my book and have picked up some useful tips. Again, I just want to stress to you that, when it comes to stock photography in particular, the sooner you begin the better. This is because you will get better and better images with practice, and the sooner you start building your library the better also.

I also wanted to quickly mention that there are several aspects of photography that I have not covered in this book, like the use of software to manipulate images. There are, however, bounds of books on these vast subjects themselves. In my opinion, it would be worth looking into some of these or attending a course on a software such as Photoshop (PS), as this will expand your skill set, especially if you would like to consider studio work/ modelling/ landscape photography/ fine art photography etc. in the future. It is therefore worth highlighting that a substantial amount of photography work happens after the photograph is taken through the process of manipulation. Expert photographers can precisely alter images to fulfil the client's brief as part of the editing process. Therefore, learning the basics of this skill will put you in great stead for advancing your photography and potential income.

In terms of stock photography itself, do not be tempted to think that it is a "get rich quick" business. It is not. Sales will come. Initially, they will trickle in. But slowly, they will build. Then, as the months go by, the sales will become more regular and increase in value. You will then learn how to identify the best-sellers out of your images. As your photography skills improve, so will your efficiency.

Like I have said before; the beauty of stock photography is that you can start anywhere at any time. The flexibility of photography means it can easily be fitted in around work and any other commitments. Just take some time to look around your natural surroundings and you will quickly start to notice material for your images popping up- even on your lunch break! Then when you start taking photos, you can build your image library slowly.

In hindsight, I really wish I had started stock photography 30 years ago. Imagine even submitting 50-100 images per month. That is 600-1200 per year. After 5 years, you would have a library with 3000+ images. That is simply mind blowing! With those sorts of figures, you could start to build a nice steady income from your stock photography. Then there is always the consideration to start expanding into other fields with your photography skills: press photography, portraiture and sports photography are just some of the categories that are up and coming.

So even if you are just getting into stock photography to fund the camera gear for your hobby, keep with it. Persist with the photographs, but do not expect miracles. However, hopefully you will find that my tips and short cuts help you to blossom a lot faster in this field than I did.

Therefore, I want to end this book by wishing you all the success in the world with your stock photography. Remember to be patient and never give up. Persistence is the key.

Useful companies:

Alamy (Excellent for stills)
Shutterstock (Good for video and stills)
Big Stock Photo (Stills)
Pond 5 (Good for video content)
Camerabits.com (Photo Mechanic)
istock (Good for stills)

THE END
All wording and images are:
Copyright Simon James Matthews LBIPP